T0391631

TURNING INTO A DRAGONFLY

by Tyler Gieseke

Cody Koala

An Imprint of Pop!
popbooksonline.com

abdobooks.com

Published by Pop!, a division of ABDO, PO Box 398166, Minneapolis, Minnesota 55439. Copyright ©2022 by Abdo Consulting Group, Inc. International copyrights reserved in all countries. No part of this book may be reproduced in any form without written permission from the publisher. Cody Koala™ is a trademark and logo of Pop!.

Printed in the United States of America, North Mankato, Minnesota

102021
012022

♻ **THIS BOOK CONTAINS RECYCLED MATERIALS**

Cover Photo: iStockphoto
Interior Photos: Shutterstock Images, 1–13, 17–21; WildPictures / Alamy Stock Photo, 14

Editor: Elizabeth Andrews
Series Designers: Laura Graphenteen, Victoria Bates

Library of Congress Control Number: 2021942248

Publisher's Cataloging-in-Publication Data

Names: Gieseke, Tyler, author.
Title: Turning into a dragonfly / by Tyler Gieseke
Description: Minneapolis, Minnesota : Pop!, 2022 | Series: Transforming animals | Includes online resources and index.
Identifiers: ISBN 9781098241155 (lib. bdg.) | ISBN 9781098241858 (ebook)
Subjects: LCSH: Dragonflies--Juvenile literature. | Insects--Juvenile literature. | Animal life cycles--Juvenile literature. | Insects--Metamorphosis--Juvenile literature. | Animal Behavior--Juvenile literature.
Classification: DDC 595.7--dc23

Hello! My name is

Cody Koala

Pop open this book and you'll find QR codes like this one, loaded with information, so you can learn even more!

Scan this code* and others like it while you read, or visit the website below to make this book pop.

popbooksonline.com/turn-dragonfly

*Scanning QR codes requires a web-enabled smart device with a QR code reader app and a camera.

Table of Contents

Chapter 1
Transforming Animals 4

Chapter 2
Dragonfly Eggs 8

Chapter 3
Life as a Nymph 12

Chapter 4
Taking Flight. 16

Making Connections 22
Glossary 23
Index. 24
Online Resources 24

Transforming Animals

Dragonflies dart around rivers and lakes. They are brightly colored bugs. They live all over the world. Many people think they are beautiful.

Watch a video here!

Life Cycle of a Dragonfly

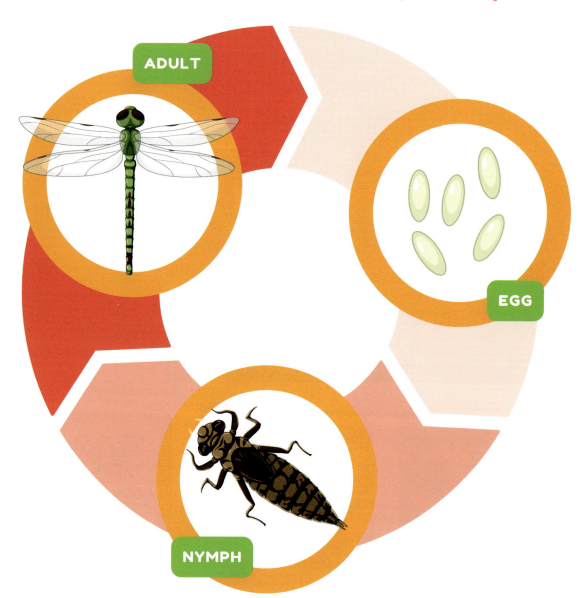

ADULT

EGG

NYMPH

Dragonflies are **transforming** animals. They grow through the dragonfly life cycle. Its three steps are egg, nymph, and adult.

Adult dragonflies have four wings. They have six legs and two eyes.

Chapter 2

Dragonfly Eggs

Dragonflies start life as eggs. Female dragonflies put their eggs in the water. Some put them in plant stems or wood.

Dragonflies have been on Earth for at least 300 million years.

adult

eggs

Female dragonflies can lay hundreds of eggs. The eggs are small and round. The eggs **hatch** after a few weeks. Then, the next step of the cycle begins!

Chapter 3

Life as a Nymph

Dragonflies are called nymphs when they **hatch**. They live underwater and breathe using **gills**. Nymphs are usually a dull color. They are only a few inches long.

Complete an activity here!

Nymphs are **predators**.
They hunt and eat small
water animals. These include
tadpoles and small fish.

Nymphs have a hard shell that covers their bodies. They **molt** this shell as they grow. Nymphs molt between five and 14 times. This takes a few years.

Nymphs will even eat other dragonfly nymphs.

Chapter 4

Taking Flight

A nymph becomes an adult dragonfly during its final **molt**. This happens above the water. It is called emergence.

Learn more here!

Emergence takes about 12 hours from start to end.

The nymph grips a plant stem. Then it breaks out of its old shell. The dragonfly waits for its new shell to dry. Its wings unfold for the first time!

Adult dragonflies fly away from water to find food. They eat other insects. Then they return to the water to **mate**.

An adult dragonfly lives for only one to six weeks. During this time, females lay their eggs. The life cycle starts again! Dragonflies are amazing **transforming** animals.

Making Connections

Text-to-Self

Which is your favorite step in the dragonfly life cycle? Why?

Text-to-Text

Have you read other books about bugs? How are those bugs similar to dragonflies? How are they different?

Text-to-World

What is another transforming animal you know about? How is its life cycle similar to or different from a dragonfly's?

Glossary

gills – body parts that help animals breathe water.

hatch – to break out of an egg.

mate – to create new eggs or babies with a partner.

molt – to shed.

predator – an animal that hunts other animals for food.

tadpole – the name for some small water animals before they become adults.

transform – to change into a new shape.

Index

color, 4, 12

eggs, 6–8, 11, 20

food, 14–15, 19

life cycle, 6–7, 11, 20

mating, 19

shell, 15, 19

water, 4, 8, 12, 15–16, 19

wings, 7, 19

Online Resources

popbooksonline.com

Thanks for reading this Cody Koala book!

Scan this code* and others like it in this book, or visit the website below to make this book pop!

popbooksonline.com/turn-dragonfly

*Scanning QR codes requires a web-enabled smart device with a QR code reader app and a camera.